THE ROYAL YEAR

A Present-Day Portrait of the Royal Family

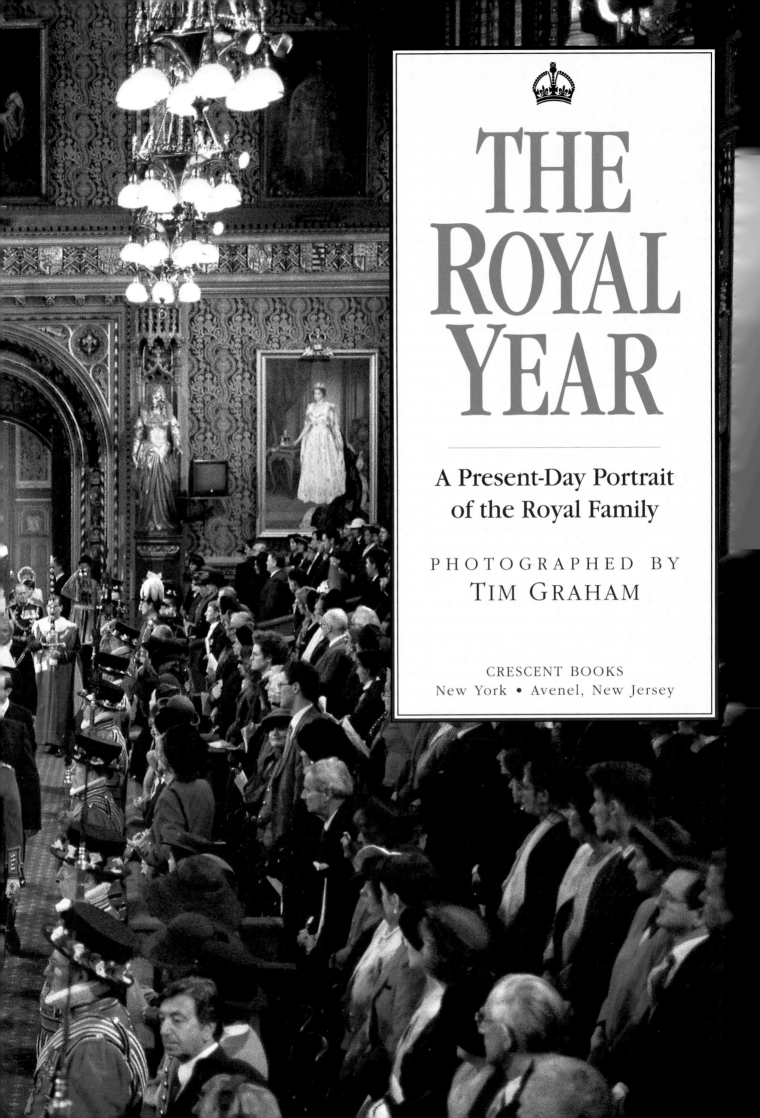

THE ROYAL YEAR

A Present-Day Portrait of the Royal Family

PHOTOGRAPHED BY
TIM GRAHAM

CRESCENT BOOKS
New York • Avenel, New Jersey

This 1994 edition published by Crescent Books,
distributed by Random House Value Publishing, Inc.,
40 Engelhard Avenue, Avenel, New Jersey 07001
by arrangement with Michael O'Mara Books Limited, London

Copyright © 1994 by Tim Graham

Random House
New York • Toronto • London • Sydney • Auckland

A CIP catalog record for this book is available
from the Library of Congress

Designed and typeset by Martin Bristow
Edited by Fiona Holman

Printed and bound in Italy by C.R. Officine Grafiche de Agostini

*Page 1: The Imperial State
Crown, with its most historic
jewel, the gleaming Black
Prince's ruby, is just one of
the many magnificent Crown
Jewels on display in the new
Jewel House at the Tower of
London which was opened by
the Queen in March.*
*Page 2: The Queen and Prince
Philip processing through the
Royal Gallery on their way to the
Chamber of the House of Lords at
the State Opening of Parliament
in November, an occasion of
pageantry and historic meaning.*
*Right: On 29 June the Princess of
Wales, as Patron of The Trust for
Sick Children in Wales, attended
the gala opening night of the Kirov
Ballet performing* Romeo and
Juliet *at the London Coliseum.*
*Far right: The Princess of Wales
is Patron of the Institute for the
Study of Drug Dependence and
on 22 June she attended the
ISDD Media Awards Lunch in
central London. During the ceremony the Princess was herself
presented with a special award
for her success in conveying some
fundamental insights into drug
misuse to a wide audience.*

On 25 June the Queen visited Tidworth in Hampshire for the Amalgamation Parade and Presentation of the Guidon to The Queen's Royal Lancers. As Colonel-in-Chief of the new regiment, which was the result of merging two historic regiments dating from the seventeenth and eighteenth centuries, the Queen reviewed the drive past and inspected the men on parade.

On 23 June the Duke and Duchess of York made a rare public appearance together to watch their elder daughter, Princess Beatrice compete in the Upton House School Sports Day. Princess Eugenie sat with her parents to watch the events and also took part in the toddlers' race.

In July the Queen traditionally
moves to Edinburgh to carry out
a week of official engagements in
Scotland, which always includes
a garden party held at the Palace
of Holyroodhouse, the Queen's
official residence in Scotland.
Right: The Queen accompanied
by Captain General and Gold
Stick for Scotland Colonel the
Lord Clydesmuire at the garden
party on 1 July.
Below: During the week in
Scotland several members of the
royal family join the Queen to
help undertake the many engagements. Seen here are the Prince of
Wales and the Princess Royal
arriving at the garden party.

Facing page: On 6 July the
Queen officially unveiled the
nation's tribute to the Queen
Mother, the Queen Elizabeth
Gate in Hyde Park.
Above right: The Queen with
Prince Michael of Kent who
masterminded the appeal to raise
the funds to pay for the gate from
public donations.
Above far right: Princess Michael
of Kent and Lord Frederick
Windsor watch the official
unveiling.
Below: The Queen and Queen
Mother take a closer look at the
design, which included emblems
illustrating the Queen Mother's
life – a leaping salmon to mark
her love of fishing and a peacock
to mark her role as the last
Empress of India.

In July the Princess of Wales
paid a visit to Zimbabwe to carry
out engagements for several of
her favourite charities, the Red
Cross, the Leprosy Mission and
Help the Aged.
*Facing page: The Princess of
Wales ladling out bean and nut
stew to the pupils of Nemazuwa
School who are all fed by the Red
Cross.*
*Below: On the last day of the
tour the Princess of Wales visited
the Tongogara Refugee Camp
near Zimbabwe's border with
Mozambique.*

In July the Princess of Wales took
Prince Harry with her on a visit
to the Light Dragoons' Barracks
at Wisden in Germany.
Facing page above: The Princess
of Wales and Prince Harry
inspect the troops.
Below and facing page below:
After the formal duties were com-
pleted Prince Harry donned a set
of specially made army fatigues
and took control of a Scimitar
tank as well as learning how to
fire advanced weaponry.

Left: Prince Edward's well-known love of real tennis, the oldest of all the racket games, was put to the test on 18 September when he stepped onto Holyport Real Tennis Court in Berkshire where he played for thirteen hours. The prince was playing in aid of The Summer Challenge, a joint fund-raising scheme for The Lord's Taverners and The Duke of Edinburgh's Award Scheme. Facing page: Prince Edward played a series of one-set matches against well-known opponents including the actor Simon McCorkindale.

Below left: On 20 September the Duchess of Kent launched the National Almshouse Week at The Charterhouse in central London. Below right: The Princess of Wales, as Patron of Centrepoint, Soho, at the opening of the Mother and Baby project in south-east London.

Right: The Princess of Wales arriving at the West London Mission in central London on 13 September.
Below: Viscount Linley and his fiancée the Hon Serena Stanhope at the official launch for his book Classical Furniture *at Sotheby's in London's West End on 15 September.*

Facing page: The Prince of Wales holding two walking sticks he had received earlier that afternoon as gifts for playing polo at Cirencester Park.

Right: Princess Margaret at the official opening of the Minnie Kidd House in Clapham, south London on 21 September.
Below left: The Princess of Wales was guest of honour at the Gala Opening of the new Warner West End Cinema in Leicester Square on 23 September after a multi-million pound rebuilding programme.
Below right: The Duchess of Gloucester, Patron, at the official opening of the Bobath Centre in East Finchley, north London on 1 October. The Centre now has the largest purpose-built premises in Europe for the treatment of children with cerebral palsy.

Facing page left: Princess Margaret, Patron of the Friends of St John's, Smith Square, visited the church on 5 October for a gala concert to inaugurate the new Sainsbury organ.
Facing page right: The Princess of Wales, Patron of the London Symphony Chorus, went to the Barbican Centre on 6 October for a performance of Mozart's Requiem.

The society wedding of the year was held at St Margaret's Church, Westminster on 8 October when Princess Margaret's son Viscount Linley married the Hon Serena Stanhope, Irish-born heiress and daughter of Viscount Petersham. *Facing page above left:* The Queen arriving at St Margaret's. *Facing page above right:* The Princess of Wales talking to the clergy outside the church door. *Facing page below:* Lord Snowdon and Princess Margaret arriving with their daughter Lady Sarah Armstrong-Jones. *Right:* The Princess Royal wore peacock blue silk at the wedding. *Below left:* Arriving for her grandson's wedding the Queen Mother was escorted to the church door by Prince Edward. *Below right:* Last year's royal bride, Lady Helen Taylor and her husband Mr Tim Taylor arriving at the church.

Facing page: After the wedding service the bride and groom, Viscount and Viscountess Linley, emerged from St Margaret's to face the cheering crowds. The bride's stunning dress of oyster duchesse satin and stiffened tulle was a tribute to Princess Margaret who had worn a similar dress at her own wedding to Lord Snowdon in 1960.

Left: On 12 October the Princess of Wales, Patron, British Red Cross Youth, attended a Royal Gala performance of La Bohème *at the London Coliseum in aid of the British Red Cross appeal for victims of war in former Yugoslavia.*

Right: On 14 October the Princess of Wales, Patron, the Leprosy Mission, presented Special Service Awards to mission volunteers at Lambeth Palace, the official residence of the Archbishop of Canterbury.

Below: With Dr George Carey, the Archbishop of Canterbury.

The Queen and Prince Philip paid a visit to Cyprus in late October to attend the Commonwealth Heads of Government meeting and to visit British forces stationed there. The visit was the first by a British monarch since Richard the Lionheart landed on the island in 1191.
Right: The Queen on her visit to the Curium Amphitheatre near Limassol on 21 October.
Below: The official group photograph of the Queen with the Commonwealth Heads of Delegation on board HM Yacht Britannia. The President of Cyprus is seated between the Queen and Prince Philip.

Right: The Queen inspecting the UN guard of honour during her visit to Wayne's Keep Commonwealth Cemetery in the UN Buffer Zone.

Facing page: A relaxing moment for the Queen in the sunshine at the Curium Amphitheatre.
Above: Prince Philip visited the UN Headquarters on 22 October.
Right: The Queen talking to children at RAF Akrotiri.

On 25 October the Princess of Wales, Patron of Help the Aged, paid a one-day visit to Brussels to carry out engagements as part of the European Year of Solidarity with the Elderly.
Left: The Princess of Wales took tea with King Baudouin's widow, Queen Fabiola at Laeken Palace.
Below: At Laeken Palace with (from left to right) Queen Fabiola, Princess Astrid and the Queen of the Belgians, wife of King Baudouin's successor, King Albert.
Facing page: The Princess of Wales at the HelpAge International Offices in Brussels.

The Prince of Wales went to Oxford on 27 October to carry out several engagements including, as Patron, visiting the Oxford Centre for Islamic Studies.
Right: Meeting children after his arrival on the edge of Oxford by helicopter.
Below: The Prince of Wales outside the Sheldonian Theatre, accompanied by the Chancellor of Oxford University, Lord Jenkins.

Facing page right: The Duchess of York arriving for the Stay Alive Ball at the Marriott Hotel on 4 November.
Facing page far right: The Princess of Wales, Patron, British Red Cross Youth, being greeted by Lord Archer as she arrived at the Mirabelle Restaurant in central London. The Princess was attending a lunch hosted by Lord Archer in honour of the 1993 British Red Cross Care in Crisis Award winners.
Facing page below: Prince Edward, Patron, the Lord's Taverners, arriving at Simpson's-in-the-Strand for the Young Lord's Taverners Masked Ball on 18 November.

In November the King and Queen of Malaysia, the Yang di-Pertuan Agong and the Raja Permaisuri Agong paid a State Visit to the Queen and Prince Philip. On 11 November the Yang di-Pertuan Agong hosted the customary Return Banquet at the Dorchester Hotel, London. The royal ladies turned out in force in full evening dress with glittering jewellery, including the royal family orders.

Facing page above left: The Duchess of Gloucester.

Facing page above right: Princess Michael of Kent.

Facing page below left: Princess Alexandra, the Hon Lady Ogilvy.

Facing page below right: The Duchess of Kent.

Left: The Queen arriving at the Dorchester Hotel.

Right: The Princess of Wales in emerald green and wearing the Spencer tiara.

Below: On the first evening of the Yang di-Pertuan Agong's State Visit the Queen held a State Banquet at Buckingham Palace. (From left to right) The Queen Mother, the King and Queen of Malaysia and the Queen.

The Princess of Wales visited Wales on 16 November to carry out a series of engagements in Carmarthen. Here she is seen at the Teen Challenge in Gorslas where she visited a crafts workshop and met staff and students.

On Remembrance Day, 14 November, the Queen led the annual service of commemoration at the Cenotaph in Whitehall, London to honour the nation's war victims and survivors.
Facing page far left: Remembrance Day was also the 45th birthday of the Prince of Wales, seen here in naval uniform in front of the Cenotaph.
Facing page left: Prince Philip, in army uniform, laid his wreath on the Cenotaph after the Queen.
Facing page below: Members of the royal family watching the Cenotaph service from the windows of the Foreign and Commonwealth Office building. (From left to right) Commander Laurence, the Duke of Gloucester, the Princess Royal and the Queen Mother.

Left: The Queen lays the first wreath at the Cenotaph.
Below: The Remembrance Sunday service is a moving occasion, with detachments of serving men and women from the forces and ex-servicemen and women lined up around the Cenotaph. Solemn music played by the Massed Bands and Pipers, the choir of the Chapel Royal and the sound of Big Ben booming out along Whitehall at 11 o'clock are traditional highlights of the service.

The Queen went in State to the House of Lords at Westminster on 18 November for the State Opening of Parliament.
Right: While her coach and mounted escort makes its way from Buckingham Palace to the Palace of Westminster the Imperial State Crown is carried to the Robing Room to await the Queen's arrival.
Facing page: After the Queen has put on the State Robes and the Imperial State Crown the magnificent procession walks slowly through the Royal Gallery to the Chamber of the House of Lords. In the procession, the Lord Great Chamberlain and the Earl Marshal traditionally walk backwards before the monarch.
Below: The Queen is accompanied by Prince Philip.

Facing page above left: The Queen visited Winchester in Hampshire on 19 November to attend a Service of Thanksgiving for the 900th anniversary of the city's cathedral.

Facing page above right: The Princess of Wales, Patron, National Aids Trust, attended the Concert of Hope at Wembley Arena to commemorate World Aids Day on 1 December.

Facing page below: Being introduced to the singer George Michael who organized the Wembley concert.

Right and below: The Princess of Wales, Patron of the Headway National Head Injuries Association, making her speech at a lunch held at the London Hilton Hotel on 3 December. It was during this speech that the Princess announced her decision to retire from public life at the end of the year in order to devote more time to bringing up her children.

Left: The Duchess of York taking part at the Children of Science party at the House of Commons on 9 December.
Below: The Princess of Wales being greeted by royal fan, Colin Edwards when she attended the opening of the St Matthew's Community Centre at the Elephant and Castle, south London on 10 December.
Facing page: The Duke and Duchess of York leaving Upton House School with Princess Beatrice and Princess Eugenie after Princess Beatrice's end-of-term Christmas play.

Right: Princess Michael of Kent, Patron of Sparks (Sport Aiding Medical Research for Children), at the 1993 Sparks Ball on 13 December.
Below: The Prince of Wales on walkabout when he visited east London on 15 December to attend the launch of the Prince's Trust's new education initiative.

Facing page above: The Princess of Wales, Patron of Centrepoint, Soho, being showered with presents of flowers as she left the AGM and 25th Anniversary launch at the Institute of Contemporary Art, central London on 16 December.
Facing page below: The Duchess of York held a signing session of her new book Travels with Queen Victoria *at Hatchards Bookshop in Piccadilly on 21 December.*

*Facing page: Belgravia Police
Station in central London was
formally opened by one of its
most famous residents, the
Princess Royal on 13 January.
Right: The Duke of York enjoy-
ing a joke during his visit to the
Barrowmore Village Settlement
Nursing Home at Great Barrow
near Chester, one of the engage-
ments he carried out in Cheshire
on 12 January.
Below: The Duchess of Kent with
Cardinal Hume at Archbishop's
House, beside Westminster
Cathedral, after she was received
into the Roman Catholic Church
at a private Mass on 14 January.
She is the first member of the
royal family to convert to
Catholicism since the famous
1701 Act of Settlement.*

In January the Prince of Wales made a three-week visit to Australia and New Zealand. By the end of the highly successful tour the Prince of Wales seemed more relaxed than he had for months and public interest had been high. The crowds in Australia were larger than expected, especially following the security scare in Sydney when his calm reaction to an armed protester won him universal admiration.

Right: The Prince of Wales keeping cool on Australia Day, 26 January, during his visit to the Carnivale Community Day at Parramatta Park, Sydney.

Below: Earlier in the day the Prince visited the Phuoc Hue Buddhist Temple in Wetherill Park, Sydney.

Facing page above: Touring the Sydney Olympic Games (2000) site at Homebush.

Facing page below left: On a visit to Deep Gorge, an Aboriginal Heritage Site near Karratha in Western Australia, Prince Charles encountered temperatures up to 50°C.

Facing page below right: Playing pool in Perth on 31 January.

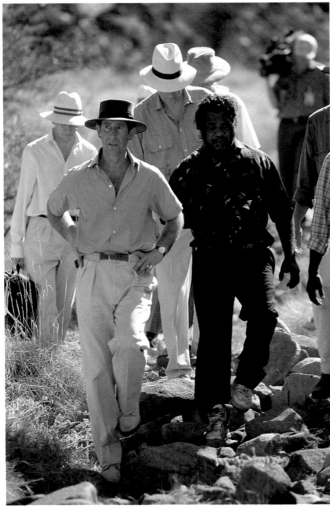

Left: Rubbing noses or exchanging a hongi *is a traditional Maori greeting and on Waitangi Day Prince Charles joined in Maori celebrations at Marae Ground. Waitangi Day is the annual commemoration of the treaty under which the Maoris ceded sovereignty of New Zealand to Queen Victoria in return for a perpetual guarantee of their historic land rights.*

Below: Driving back from a visit to the organically run Ngaioti Farm, Prince Charles stopped on the road to allow a local resident to photograph him with her children.

Facing page above left: At Waitekere City meeting members of the Waiperera Trust and Maori warriors.

Facing page above right: Playing cricket at Fendalton Primary School, Christchurch.

Facing page below: Prince Charles wearing the traditional Maori elder's feather cloak and holding two sacred sticks at Turangawaewae Marae.

Facing page above left: The Prince of Wales arriving at Zurich Airport with his two sons at the start of their short half-term skiing holiday in Klosters, Switzerland.
Facing page above right: Prince Harry holding his skis.
Facing page below: Prince Charles and Prince William armed with skis and goggles.
Right: After three action-packed days the young princes returned to school in England and the Prince of Wales then spent an afternoon indulging in one of his favourite pastimes, painting watercolours in the outdoors.
Below: The Prince of Wales and Prince William take a chairlift together above Klosters.

Facing page: The Prince of Wales and the young princes in brilliant sunshine at Klosters. Determined to enjoy his sons' company to the full during their brief holiday together Prince Charles skied with them all day on easier blue runs rather than tackling his more normal, difficult black runs. Right: Princess Michael of Kent in dazzling deep blue velvet evening wear for the Horse and Hound *Ball at the Grosvenor House Hotel on 3 March.*

Right and below left: Following a bout of flu in January the Queen Mother made her first public appearance for two months at the National Hunt Festival, the climax of the winter racing calendar, which takes place each year at Cheltenham.

Below right and facing page: On St Patrick's Day, 17 March, the Queen Mother made her traditional presentation of shamrocks to the Irish Guards at Chelsea Barracks, London. The Queen Mother first carried out this duty as Duchess of York in 1926.

Left: The Princess Royal, Commander Laurence and Peter Phillips at the Gatcombe Novice Horse Trials held at Gatcombe Park, the Princess's Gloucestershire home on 20 March.
Below: Home from school for the Easter holidays Peter Phillips was keen to help with the Horse Trials. Here he is driving a tractor around the park with his sister Zara and a friend in the trailer behind.
Facing page above left: Peter Phillips is now a pupil at Gordonstoun School, Scotland, where his grandfather Prince Philip and the Princess Royal's three brothers were all pupils.
Facing page below: Zara Phillips walking her dog during the Horse Trials.

Right: Prince William arriving at Zurich Airport on his way to Lech in Austria for an Easter skiing holiday with the Princess of Wales and his younger brother Prince Harry.
Below: The Princess of Wales helping Prince Harry to put on his skis.

Facing page: Prince William (left) and Prince Harry (right) who are now both keen skiers.

Left: The Princess of Wales skiing.
Facing page above: The Princess of Wales on a chairlift with her friend Kate Menzies.
Facing page below: Taking a horse-drawn sleigh to the nearby village of Zug for supper. Looking more and more relaxed as the holiday progressed the Princess of Wales was determined to enjoy every moment with the young princes.
Overleaf: The royal skiing party posing for photographers on the second day of the holiday.

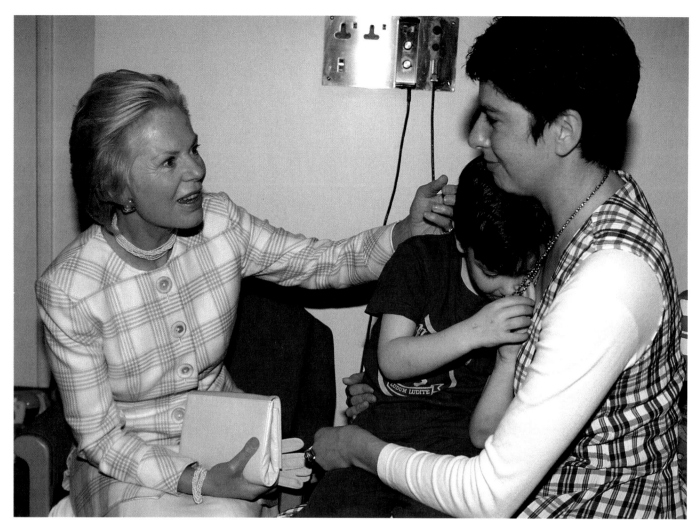

Above: The Duchess of Kent meeting patients during her visit to the Royal Free Hospital in north London on 22 April to open new facilities for haemophilia care and research.

Right: Prince Edward was accompanied by his girlfriend Sophie Rhys-Jones to his cousin Lord Ivar Mountbatten's wedding on 23 April at Clare in Suffolk. Below and facing page below: Princess Margaret accompanied her nephew Prince Edward and Sophie Rhys-Jones to the church.

Far left: The Duchess of Kent at the Scouts' St George's Day Parade in the Great Quadrangle of Windsor Castle on 24 April. Left: The Princess of Wales, Patron, went to Drapers' Hall in the city of London on 27 April to attend a lunch celebrating the 10th anniversary of the Help the Hospices Association.

Right: The Queen arriving at the Jockey Club in Newmarket, Suffolk on 25 April. Newmarket is the historic capital of flat racing, one of the Queen's favourite hobbies, and during her visit to the town she carried out several engagements connected with racing.

Facing page above: Lady Sarah Armstrong-Jones, Princess Margaret's daughter, announced her engagement to Mr Daniel Chatto on 5 May.
Facing page below: The Duchess of Kent, Patron, meeting children dressed in their national costume when she opened the 35th International Spring Fair in aid of the ISS UK at Kensington Town Hall on 11 May.

Right: The Queen with President Mitterand at Calais in northern France for the official opening ceremony of the Channel Tunnel, linking Britain to Europe for the first time since the last Ice Age 10,000 years ago.
Below: The Queen and Prince Philip with the President of France and Madame Mitterand in front of a Eurostar train at the opening ceremony.

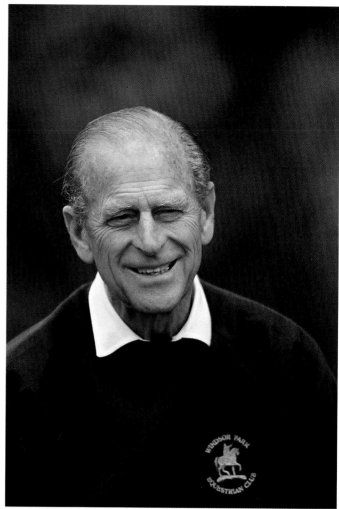

May's Royal Windsor Horse Show is always well attended by the royal family, including this year the Duke of York (above left), the Duchess of York (facing page below left) and (above) Prince Edward, seen here talking to the Queen.

As well as Prince Philip (facing page above right), this year's royal competitors included Princess Beatrice (left) and Princess Eugenie (facing page below right) who enjoyed their candyfloss after taking part in a pony class in the show ring.

Above: Prince Philip has taken
part in the carriage-driving
events at the Royal Windsor
Horse Show for many years.
He is seen here with his team of
ponies during the marathon
event in Windsor Great Park.
Left: The Queen watching from
her Land Rover.

Right: On 10 May the Prince of
Wales, Colonel-in-Chief, present-
ed the Army Air Corps with the
first guidon or ceremonial pen-
nant at a colourful ceremony at
their headquarters in Middle
Wallop, Hampshire.
Far right: The Prince of Wales,
Great Master, attended a service
for the members of the Most
Honourable Order of the Bath in
Westminster Abbey on 16 May.

Facing page: In May the Prince of Wales paid his first visit to the historic city of St Petersburg in Russia. His engagements included (above) laying a wreath at the Piskarevskoye Cemetery and (below) visiting many of the city's famous architectural sights.

This page: On 27 May the Princess of Wales flew to Geneva for meetings with the Red Cross and Red Crescent societies as a member of their new advisory commission.

Right: On 1 June the Queen went to Epsom Racecourse for Derby Day. The Queen is an enthusiastic follower of flat racing and usually brings a large party of guests to Epsom.
Below: The Queen, the Princess Royal and Prince Philip watching the racing from the royal box.

Right: On 3 June the royal family attended a ceremony in Green Park, central London for the unveiling of a memorial to the Canadian forces who took part in both World Wars. (From left to right) the Hon. Sir Angus Ogilvy, Princess Alexandra, the Duke of Kent, Princess Margaret, the Duke of York and the Princess of Wales.

Below: The Queen and Prince Philip with President Clinton at the D-Day anniversary dinner held at the Portsmouth Guildhall on 4 June. The Heads of Government of the nations which had participated in Operation Neptune, the codename for the maritime phase of the invasion of Normandy, were guests of honour at the glittering dinner.

On 5 June the heads and representatives of 12 nations joined up to 70,000 people for an eve-of-battle Drumhead Service on Southsea Common in Portsmouth to pay tribute to those who took part in D-Day.
Right: The Princess of Wales talking to Commander Laurence after the service.
Below: Prince Philip, the Queen Mother, Princess Margaret, the Princess Royal, Commander Laurence and the Princess of Wales during the Drumhead Service.

Facing page: On 6 June, the 50th anniversary of D-Day, the main British commemorative ceremony in Normandy was the Veterans' Review and Marchpast on the beach at Arromanches, the Gold beach of D-Day.
Above: The Princess Royal, Commander Laurence and the Prince of Wales at Arromanches.
Below: The Queen and Prince Philip arriving on the beach at Arromanches where the Queen took the salute from more than 7,000 veterans.

Facing page above: The Queen and Prince Philip walking among the rows of white gravestones at the Commonwealth War Cemetery in Bayeux, the largest World War II cemetery in France. Facing page below and right: After the Marchpast at Arromanches, the Queen spent some time talking to veterans before leaving the town.

Below: The Duchess of Kent talking to Chelsea Pensioners during their colourful and historic annual Founder's Day Parade at the Royal Hospital, Chelsea on 9 June. In honour of the Royal Hospital's Founder, Charles II, the Pensioners wear a bunch of oak leaves on their scarlet coats on Founder's Day.

Trooping the Colour is the historic ceremony held to mark the monarch's official birthday and during the present Queen's reign has taken place on the second Saturday in June.

Right: The Queen leaves Buckingham Palace with precisely enough time to spare so that she ends the mile-long drive to Horse Guards Parade in Whitehall on the stroke of eleven.

Below: The Queen Mother and the Duchess of Gloucester driving to Horse Guards Parade to watch the Queen's Birthday Parade.

Facing page above: The Queen at Horse Guards Parade.

Facing page below: Arriving back at Buckingham Palace, the Queen watches the King's Troop, the Royal Horse Artillery and the Household Cavalry march past.

Right: The Queen Mother, the Queen and Prince Philip on the balcony of Buckingham Palace to watch the fly-past by the Royal Air Force to mark the official celebration of the Queen's Birthday.
Below: In the royal party on the Palace balcony were (from left to right) the Queen Mother, the Duchess of Gloucester, Lord Romsey, Lady Helen Taylor, Prince Edward, Lord Brabourne and Prince and Princess Michael of Kent.
Facing page above: The crowds in front of the Palace railings enjoy a good view of the royal family on the balcony as well as the fly-past overhead.
Facing page below: Watching the fly-past from the Palace balcony were Princess Michael of Kent, the Prince of Wales, Prince Edward and Viscount and Viscountess Linley.

The Most Noble Order of the Garter is England's highest order of chivalry as well as being one of the oldest. The colourful Garter Day Ceremony takes place each year at Windsor Castle in the middle of June. The Queen is Head of the Order and this year installed the Princess Royal as a Lady Companion of the Order, one of the few female members of the royal family to be so honoured.
Facing page above: The Princess Royal returning to Windsor Castle with Commander Laurence after the Garter Day Service in St George's Chapel.
Facing page below: The Queen and Prince Philip being driven back to Windsor Castle.
Right: Wearing her blue and crimson Garter robes and the cap with its distinctive white ostrich plume for the first time, the Princess Royal walks in procession to St George's Chapel.
Below: The Queen and Prince Philip leaving St George's Chapel.

Left: The Prince of Wales kisses the Queen's hand as he receives the consolation prize after a polo match at Smith's Lawn on 15 June.
Below left: Viscountess Linley on Ladies' Day at Royal Ascot.
Below right: The Queen Mother wearing bright yellow for Royal Ascot.

Facing page above left: The Princess of Wales arriving at the Serpentine Gallery in Kensington Gardens on 29 June for a gala fundraising dinner.
Facing page above right and below: Prince Charles went to Caernarvon Castle in north Wales on 1 July to celebrate the twenty-fifth anniversary of his investiture as Prince of Wales by the Queen.

The wedding of Lady Sarah Armstrong-Jones to Mr Daniel Chatto took place quietly on 14 July at St Stephen Walbrook, a small Wren church in the City of London.

Facing page above left: The Queen and Prince Philip arriving at the church.

Facing page above right: The crowds outside the church gave Prince Edward and his girlfriend Sophie Rhys-Jones a loud cheer.

Facing page below: Lady Sarah Armstrong-Jones arriving at the church with her bridesmaids.

Above left: The Princess of Wales leaving the church after the wedding service.

Above right: The bride and groom outside the church.

Right: Lady Sarah's parents, Princess Margaret and the Earl of Snowdon outside the church.

Overleaf: The bride and groom.